# ARAB-ISRAELI WARS

A Cherrytree Book

Designed and produced by
A S Publishing

First published 1991
by Cherrytree Press Ltd
a subsidiary of
The Chivers Company Ltd
Windsor Bridge Road
Bath, Avon BA2 3AX

Copyright © Cherrytree Press Ltd 1991

*British Library Cataloguing in Publication Data*
Hills, Ken
    Arab-Israeli wars.
    1. Arab countries. Conflict with Israel, 1945-1991
    I. Title    II. Series
    956.04

    ISBN 0-7451-5125-6

Printed in Italy by New Interlitho, Milan

# ARAB-ISRAELI WARS

*By* Ken Hills
*Illustrated by* Neil Reed

CHERRYTREE BOOKS

# The Roots of Conflict

Arabs and Jews have been in conflict almost without ceasing since the state of Israel was founded in 1948. Since then, the two sides have fought four major wars and untold minor battles. Today there is still little prospect of peace between them.

The country known to the Jews as Israel, and to the Arabs as Palestine, is in the Middle East. The Middle East commands the shortest, quickest and cheapest route by sea (via the Suez Canal) from Europe to Australia and South East Asia. The area holds colossal reserves of oil. It is the birthplace of three major religions: Judaism, Christianity and Islam.

The conflict between Jews and Arabs is that both claim the land of Palestine as their own. To the Jews, the land they have named Israel is their ancient home. They claim

David, King of the Jews, made Jerusalem his capital around 1000 BC. Since then it has been fought over and captured by Assyrians, Romans, Arabs, Turks, Crusaders, Egyptians and the British. Signs of the continuing conflict are visible in many areas of the city.

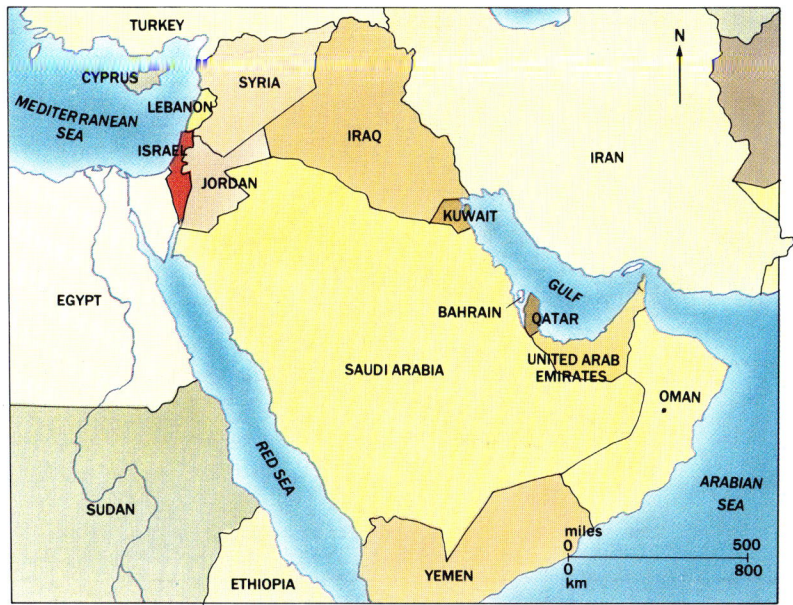

About 140 million people live in the Middle East. Of the historic land of Palestine, most now belongs to Israel, and the rest to Jordan, Lebanon and Syria.

that it was theirs for a thousand years until the Romans conquered it and, in AD 135, destroyed Jerusalem and drove them out. The Jews scattered around the world, but wherever they went and in spite of hideous persecution they preserved their faith and their customs. Always, they nursed the hope of returning to their homeland and of worshipping once again in Jerusalem.

The Arabs conquered Palestine in the seventh century AD. They were converted to Islam, and Jerusalem became one of their most holy places. Palestine was an Arab land for centuries until, in 1948, Jews who had settled there from all over the world set up the state of Israel. Hundreds of thousands of Arabs fled and became refugees in neighbouring Arab states. To these Arabs, Palestine is their native land and they are determined to fight to regain it.

### DREAMS OF ZION

Theodor Herzl was born in 1860, the son of a wealthy Jewish banker. He grew up in Austria, and became convinced that Jews would only be safe from the persecution they had suffered down the ages if they established an independent Jewish state. Herzl set out his beliefs, in 1896, in a book called 'The Jewish State'. Other Jews developed his ideas. The desire for a Jewish state grew into the Zionist movement, so called after Mount Zion on which ancient Jerusalem was built.

# Britain and Palestine

World War I, 1914-18, was a turning point in the history of Palestine. At the time, most of the Middle East and the Arabs who lived there were ruled by Turkey. When Turkey came into the war on the German side, against Britain, the British gave their support to anyone who would join them in the fight against the Turks. Through their agent T.E. Lawrence, the British encouraged the Arab revolt of 1916 against their Turkish overlords.

**T.E. Lawrence's interest in the Middle East was initially as an archaeologist. In World War I, the British sent him as their agent to fight with the Arabs in their revolt against the Turks.**

## Conflicting Promises

To win the Arabs to their side, the British promised to support Arab claims to an independent state in Palestine when the war was over. The next year, the British Foreign Secretary Arthur Balfour declared in a letter to a Jewish leader that Britain favoured the establishment of a national home for the Jewish people in Palestine, and would do its best to help the Jews to set it up. Thus both the Arabs and the Jews were led to believe that Britain supported their aims in Palestine.

Turkey lost her Middle East empire in the war and it passed into the care of the League of Nations. The League entrusted Palestine to Britain to govern until the people there were capable of governing themselves.

Immediately, there was trouble between Jews and Arabs. Jews poured into Palestine and the Arabs living there foresaw that they would soon be outnumbered. The Jews confirmed their fears by stating openly their aim to set up a Jewish state. There were periodic riots between the two peoples and in 1936 the British had to put down a full-scale Arab revolt.

To try to solve the problem, the British made a proposal to divide Palestine into separate Jewish and Arab states, but it pleased no-one. In 1938 the plan for partition was abandoned.

In 1939 World War II broke out.

**Palestine is a small country and much of it is natural swamp or desert. The Jews who fled there worked ceaselessly to drain the swamps and bring water to the desert, to turn it into a land fit to live in.**

### PERSECUTION

After World War I ended, there was a steady flow of Jews who went to Palestine as settlers. After 1933 this flow became a flood, as Nazi persecution of the Jews forced thousands to flee from Europe and seek freedom and safety in Palestine. By 1939, there were seven times as many Jews in Palestine as there had been in 1918. When the extent of the Holocaust became known after World War II, sympathy for the Jews was intense.

# The Impact of War

In 1939, Britain went to war with Germany. Once again she needed Arab support, this time to safeguard supplies of oil from the Middle East, and to keep open the Suez Canal. To please the Arabs, the British agreed to limit the number of Jews coming to settle in Palestine to 75,000 over the next five years. After that, Jewish immigration would cease altogether unless the Arabs agreed that it should begin again. The Jews were bitterly hostile to this plan since there were thousands of homeless Jews in Europe resolved to come to Palestine. Nevertheless, most Jews supported Britain in the war with Germany and a number joined the British armed forces.

**On 22 July 1946 Jewish terrorists blew up the King David Hotel, the British headquarters in Jerusalem. This outrage finally convinced the British that they should leave Palestine.**

On 14 May 1948, in Tel Aviv, David Ben-Gurion, the Prime Minister, declared Israel independent. That same evening, Israel was invaded by Arab armies from Egypt, Transjordan (now Jordan) and Lebanon. They came determined to defend the rights of their fellow Arabs in Palestine, and to crush the new state out of existence.

The flag of Israel shows the Star of David and its colours are those of the traditional shawl which Jews wear at prayer.

## The Post-war Conflict

When World War II ended in 1945, Britain faced a renewed conflict in Palestine. Jewish terrorist groups, such as the Stern Gang and the Irgun, waged a guerilla war on the British forces. There were continual skirmishes between Jews and Arabs, and more and more British troops and police had to be drafted in to prevent open warfare from breaking out. Their reward was to be shot at by both sides.

It became clear to the British authorities that they were incapable of solving the Palestine problem and that they could no longer afford the cost in lives and resources of attempting to govern the country. On 14 February 1947 the British Foreign Secretary Ernest Bevin announced that Britain was handing the affairs of Palestine over to the United Nations.

## The British Leave

The United Nations followed the same path as the British. In November 1947 they produced a plan for dividing Palestine into two independent states: one Arab, one Jewish, with the capital Jerusalem remaining under international control. The Jews accepted the proposals, for they were given what they wanted, a land of their own. The Arabs rejected the plan, and both sides began to prepare for a war that now seemed inevitable.

The British gradually abandoned their positions in Palestine. As they left, Jews and Arabs fought to take over the vacant areas. Innocent civilians of both sides were caught up in the confusion. Arabs killed Jews, and Jews killed Arabs in the struggle for the land. On 14 May 1948, the last British left. The Jews proclaimed the state of Israel. Within hours, the Arab powers invaded.

# The Palestine War (1948)

Israel was invaded by armies from Egypt, Transjordan, Iraq, Syria and Lebanon. After a month's confused fighting a ceasefire was arranged by the UN mediator Count Folke Bernadotte. The truce rescued Israel, for she had run out of supplies needed to continue the fighting. In their new state, the Israelis had no means of manufacturing arms and ammunition. Israeli funds were exhausted so the government sent one of its leading members, Golda Meir, to the United States to raise money for the Israeli cause from America's large Jewish community. Mrs Meir knew America well; she had grown up there. In four weeks, she collected over 50 million dollars and Israel was saved.

Fighting resumed in July, and once again Bernadotte arranged a truce. In September he was shot by Jewish extremists who believed he was favouring the Arab cause.

Syrian troops moving into position against the Israelis on the Golan Heights. The Arabs outnumbered the Jews, but lost this advantage when their armies failed to co-operate.

War broke out again in October and the Israelis began to get the upper hand. By the end of the month, they had cleared Arab forces out of Galilee in the north and had forced Lebanon out of the war. Ignoring UN pleas for a ceasefire, the Israelis turned south and drove the Egyptians out of Palestine. They trapped an Egyptian army near Gaza and other Israeli units reached the Red Sea. By early 1949 all sides were ready for peace. On February 24 Egypt signed an armistice with Israel. Other Arab states followed.

The gains Israel made during the war gave her three-quarters of Palestine. There was so little left to the Arabs that there was no question of setting up an Arab state. Egypt took Gaza in the south, and an area to the west of the River Jordan known as the West Bank went to Transjordan. Jerusalem was divided between Transjordan and Israel.

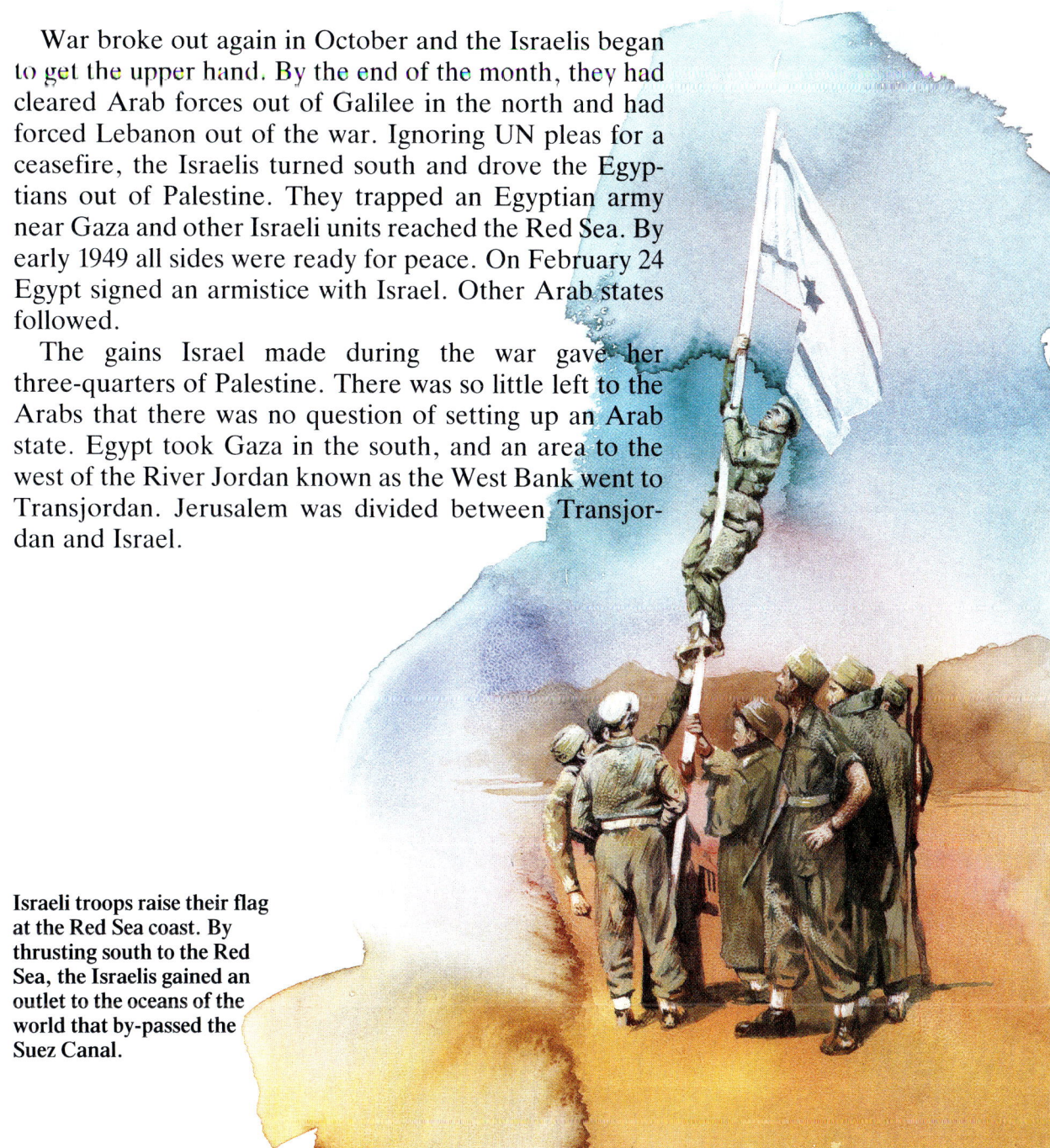

**Israeli troops raise their flag at the Red Sea coast. By thrusting south to the Red Sea, the Israelis gained an outlet to the oceans of the world that by-passed the Suez Canal.**

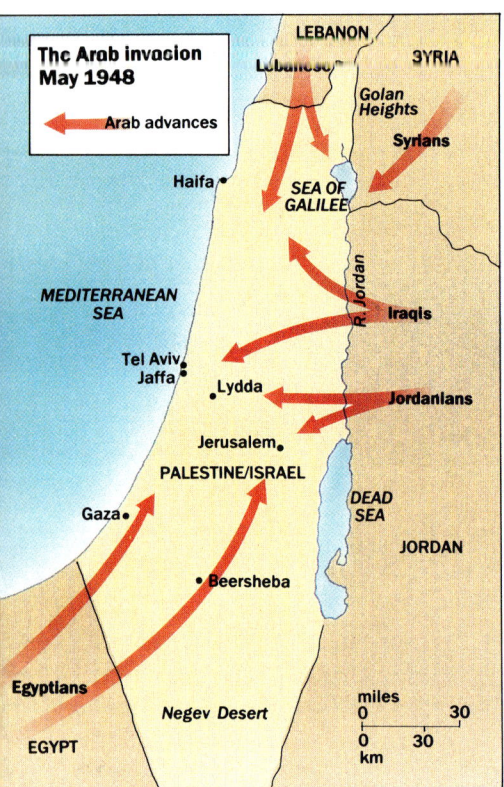

The Israelis gained three-quarters of Palestine in the war. Only the Gaza strip, the West Bank and part of Jerusalem remained in Arab hands. But Israel was hardly secure. Near Tel Aviv the country was only 15 kilometres wide. A surprise attack could easily cut it in two.

# Peace and its Problems

The war solved nothing and the viciousness of much of the fighting only made Arabs and Jews distrust each other more. The Arab states refused to recognize the new nation of Israel, and both they and the Israelis regarded the truce they had signed as no more than a pause in the struggle. But the war had improved Israel's chances of survival. Not only had she gained valuable territory, but the Israeli armed forces had learned much from the conflict. They would use these lessons to good effect in future battles.

## REFUGEES

The United Nations estimated that 656,000 Arabs fled from Palestine to the neighbouring Arab states. They left either to escape the fighting, or as a result of the post-war division of Palestine. Over half sought refuge in Transjordan (now Jordan) or the West Bank. They became people without a country, forced to live in poverty and squalor. The number of Arabs who remained in Israel was reduced to a mere 160,000.

### Seeking Refuge

The war made worse a problem which lies at the heart of the Arab-Israeli conflict: the problem of the Palestinian refugees. Palestinian Arabs fled in their thousands to escape the war. They flooded into neighbouring Arab states where they settled in shanty towns strung along the borders with Israel. Increasingly groups of these refugees, called 'Fedayeen' by the Arabs, became involved in border incidents and local disputes with the Israelis.

The movement of the refugees was not all one way. About half a million Jews lived in the Arab countries of the Middle East. The conflict forced them to leave their homes and most sought refuge in Israel, where they were welcomed as a valuable addition to the state.

The refugee settlements became bases from which Arab guerillas struck at Israel. The Israelis retaliated by attacking the refugees' homes. On average over 5000 of these incidents took place every year.

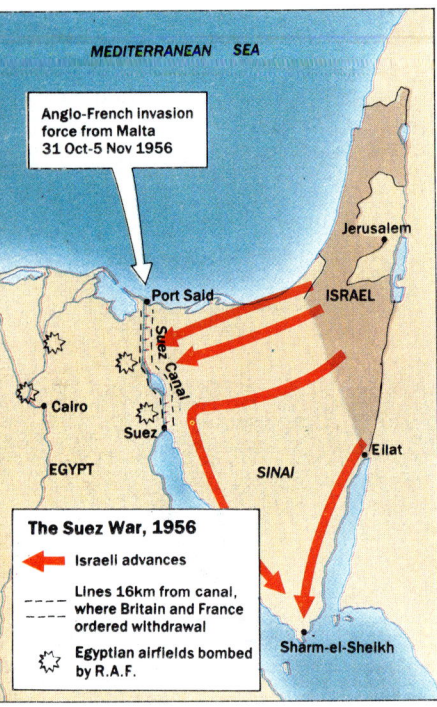

**The Suez War, 1956**

- ➡ Israeli advances
- – – – Lines 16km from canal, where Britain and France ordered withdrawal
- ✧ Egyptian airfields bombed by R.A.F.

Following the Israeli invasion of Sinai, Britain and France made a joint paratroop landing beside the canal, and the British air force bombed Egyptian airfields – much to the anger of other nations.

# The Suez War (1956)

The uneasy peace which followed lasted eight years. In Egypt President Gamal Abdel Nasser sought Soviet help to rebuild his armed forces. He re-equipped the Egyptian army, navy and air force with new weapons and promised openly that they would be used to destroy Israel. He supported Fedayeen raids into Israel and closed the Suez Canal to Israeli ships.

Nasser had approached Britain and the United States for funds to build a dam at Aswan on the River Nile to provide power and irrigation. They agreed to help but later became disillusioned with him and withdrew their

**GAMAL ABDEL NASSER**

A soldier and revolutionary, Gamal Abdel Nasser (1918-70) became President of Egypt in 1954. Under his rule, Egypt's huge estates were broken up and the land given to the peasants. To provide cheap power, he planned the Aswan High Dam. When the Western nations withdrew their aid, he seized the Suez Canal Company to help pay for it. He modernized his country but never realised his dream of uniting all Arabs, though he is remembered by them and others as a hero.

support. Nasser retaliated swiftly. On 26 July 1956 he seized the Suez Canal Company, until then owned and run by Britain and France. He announced that its huge profits would be used to pay for the Aswan Dam project. The French and British were determined to regain the canal. They co-operated with the Israelis who were greatly alarmed by Egypt's arms build-up. Secretly, the three nations prepared a plan of campaign.

The Israelis struck first. On 29 October they crossed into Sinai. The Egyptians were taken completely by surprise. By the next day the Israelis were advancing on the Suez Canal. The attack was the excuse for Britain and France to act. Pretending to protect the canal, they ordered both the Egyptians and the Israelis to withdraw from the waterway. When the Egyptians refused, the British and French invaded. Their attack was furiously condemned by world opinion. They and the Israelis were forced to withdraw, leaving Nasser triumphant and in possession of the canal.

The Israeli attack on the Egyptians in the Sinai desert was highly successful. Within a week they had captured the entire peninsula. The Israelis trapped an Egyptian army near Gaza and took many prisoners. More valuable than prisoners were the huge quantities of arms and ammunition they captured.

On the battlefield in 1967 the Arabs heavily outnumbered the Israelis. Their combined armies were twice as large and, together, they had three times as many tanks and aircraft.

Some Arab forces, such as the Jordanians, were British-trained while others, including the Egyptians, had been instructed in Russian methods.

The Israelis were a citizen army. During the week Israel's fighting men and women.went about their ordinary civilian jobs. Most weekends, they trained for war. They fought as a single force and were able to take advantage of the Arabs' differences.

# A Troubled Peace

The ten years after the Suez War were a troubled time for the Arab nations. In Iraq one revolt followed another. British influence declined and a new government of army officers favoured friendship with the Soviet Union. In 1958 Egypt and Syria combined to form the United Arab Republic, but the union broke up after three years. Iraq threatened to invade tiny Kuwait in order to grab her huge oil reserves. The Kuwaitis appealed to the West for help. A British force went in and stayed until other Arab states were ready to take over Kuwait's defence. Iraq backed off, but the incident did great harm to Arab unity.

Egyptian
Commando

Jordanian
Infantry

Israeli
Infantry

It seemed that the only matter on which the Arabs naturally agreed was the destruction of Israel. A new guerilla force drawn from the refugees, called Al Fatah, meaning 'conquest', was formed. In 1964 the Arabs set up the Palestine Liberation Organisation. It was intended to unite all the Palestinian refugees, and they agreed to give it active support.

Beginning early in 1967, clashes on the Syrian and Egyptian borders with Israel grew increasingly frequent and severe. As Arab concerns developed, Nasser was criticised at home, and by other Arab leaders, for failing to take measures to deal with a possible attack by Israel.

**Arabs throughout the Middle East showed their opposition to Israel by frequent protest marches and political demonstrations.**

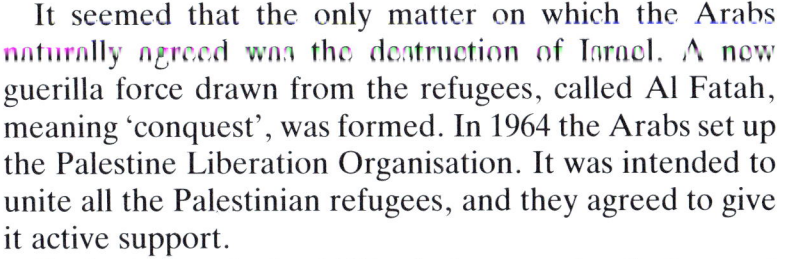

# The Six-Day War (1967)

As Arab criticism grew, Nasser realised that unless he moved quickly against the Israelis he would lose his leadership of the Arab peoples. He ordered the small UN peace-keeping force in Sinai to leave, and stopped all ships sailing to Israel's port of Eilat. He called for a Moslem holy war to destroy Israel, and massed tanks and troops on the Israeli frontier. An Egyptian attack seemed certain, but it never came. Israel struck first.

At breakfast time on 5 June 1967, without warning, Israeli aircraft appeared over Egypt's key airfields. They

Every morning, Egyptian aircraft flew dawn patrols along the Israeli frontier, and then returned to refuel. Knowing this, the Israelis timed their strike force to arrive just after these aircraft had landed, and destroyed them on the ground.

### MOSHE DAYAN

Moshe Dayan (1915-81) became a soldier in 1937. He lost an eye while fighting for the British in Syria in World War II.

Dayan was the Israeli army commander in Jerusalem during the Palestine War of 1948. He rose to be Chief of Staff and led Israeli forces in the Suez War of 1956 against Egypt. He left the army and went into politics. As Minister of Defence, he planned Israel's brilliantly successful campaign in the Six-Day War.

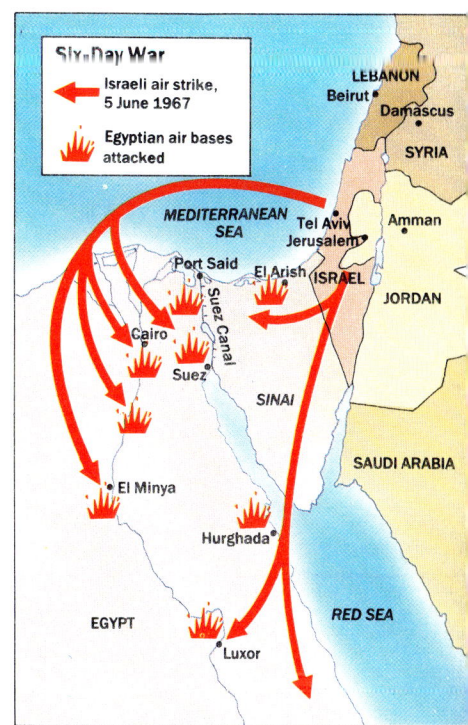

The Israeli aircraft confused the Egyptian defences by making a wide sweep out over the sea before homing in for the attack. Almost the entire Israeli air force took part in the bombing which from start to finish was over in less than three hours.

caught the Egyptian air force on the ground, and shattered it. Later the same day, in the space of a few hours, they devastated military airbases in Jordan and Syria. Israel destroyed over 400 Arab aircraft for the loss of 26 of her own and won command of the skies over the Middle East. The Arab armies on the ground were virtually without air cover. As the smoke rose from the ravaged Egyptian airfields, Israeli tanks were streaming into Sinai, immune from air attack.

The Israeli armoured columns broke through the Egyptian defences and the Egyptian armies fell back. Within six days, leading Israeli tanks had reached the Suez Canal. The entire Sinai peninsula was in Israeli hands. Jordan entered the war to relieve the hard-pressed Egyptians, but by 10 June, after some of the toughest fighting of the war, the Israelis had driven the Jordanian army out of the West Bank and occupied Jerusalem. They then turned on the Syrians who were shelling Israeli settlements from the Golan Heights. They captured the gun positions, and occupied the high ground overlooking Israel.

**Israel after the Six-Day War**

Israel, 1949-67

Israeli occupied 1967

LEBANON

SYRIA

GOLAN HEIGHTS

WEST BANK

Jerusalem

MEDITERRANEAN SEA

GAZA STRIP

ISRAEL

JORDAN

Suez Canal

SINAI

Israeli control of small oil fields

Eilat

SAUDI ARABIA

EGYPT

Sharm-el-Sheikh

The land Israel won in the war made her frontiers more secure. Sinai became a buffer against an Egyptian attack. The West Bank added width to the dangerously narrow 'waist' of the country near Tel Aviv.

# A Decisive Victory

The Israelis had won a decisive victory. It enabled them to occupy the Gaza Strip, the Sinai Peninsula to the banks of the Suez Canal, all territory west of the River Jordan and the uplands of the Golan Heights. They also seized the Old City of Jerusalem which contained places and buildings sacred both to them and the Moslem Arabs. Altogether, Israel gained 72,500 square kilometres of territory, which made it three times larger than when war broke out.

The war greatly increased the number of Palestinian Arabs under Israeli rule. Many fled to neighbouring Arab states and swelled the ranks of the refugees already there. Some 600,000 stayed in their homes in the West Bank and another 300,000 in the Gaza Strip. Their presence in the occupied territory would prove a source of endless trouble for Israel in the future.

**Fighting On**

Immediately the war was over, Israel offered to hold talks with the Arabs about the future of the Middle East. The Arab nations refused to meet the Israelis. To accept would mean that they recognized the state of Israel and its right to exist. At a conference at Khartoum, the Arab leaders pledged themselves not to make peace with the Israelis and to fight on until they had won back the land of Palestine for the Palestinian Arabs. The wealthy Arab oil-producing states of Saudi Arabia and Kuwait agreed to pay for the losses suffered by Jordan and Egypt in the war. With help from the Soviet Union, the Egyptians began to rebuild their shattered armed forces. The United States viewed Egypt's growing dependence on the Communist powers with mounting anxiety, and swiftly re armed Israel.

## War of Attrition

The Egyptians used their new weapons to harass Israel in persistent attacks along the new frontier. President Nasser proclaimed a 'war of attrition' to wear down Israeli resistance. Daily, Egyptian guns shelled Israeli positions along the Suez Canal. Daily, Israeli artillery replied. Commandos from both sides raided each others' territory, and regular air battles were fought over the border. After two years of vicious clashes, both Egyptians and Israelis had had enough. In autumn 1970 they signed a ceasefire.

Israeli guns firing on Egyptian positions across the Suez Canal. These artillery duels were regular features of the war of attrition.

# The Growth of Terror

The violence in the Middle East did not end with the ceasefire between Egypt and Israel. The Palestinian refugees were unyielding in their hostility towards Israel. They kept up an unceasing pattern of raids across Israel's frontiers, killing Israelis and destroying buildings and crops. These attacks had two purposes: to do as much damage to Israel as possible, and to keep the Palestinian cause and the plight of the Palestinian refugees on the front pages of the world's newspapers.

The leading opponent of Israel was now the Palestine Liberation Organisation led by Yasser Arafat. The PLO did not lack weapons, for the rich Arab oil states provided them with funds to buy arms. The guerillas always caused problems for the countries that sheltered them, for the Israelis invariably responded to every attack, with heavy assaults across the border on the guerilla bases.

## Black September

The PLO guerillas based themselves in Jordan. So many refugees had fled there from the fighting on the West Bank during the Six-Day War that Palestinians outnumbered the native Jordanian population. The PLO became a state within a state, and by 1970 threatened to overthrow the Jordanian government. Jordan's King Hussein attempted to curb the guerillas' growing power. They responded by provoking a civil war. After several days of bitter warfare, in September 1970, the guerilla forces were subdued by the Jordanian army and forced to leave Jordan. They set up new bases in Lebanon from which to attack Israel. The Arabs called the affair 'Black September'.

**YASSER ARAFAT**

Yasser Arafat (1928-     ) is a Palestinian born in Jerusalem. He has devoted his life to winning back a homeland in Palestine for the Palestinian people. At Cairo University, he became the leader of his fellow Palestinian students. In 1956 he formed the guerilla group Al Fatah. In 1969 he was appointed Chairman of the PLO. He is seen by many as a statesman, by others as a terrorist.

## Sadat Prepares for War

Both America and Russia urged Egypt's new leader Anwar Sadat to make peace with Israel. But Sadat refused to bargain with Israel while Egypt's position was so weak. He decided to strike a surprise blow against the Israelis which would shock them into negotiating with the Arab nations. At the same time, he planned to bring in the superpowers to impose a fair and lasting settlement of Middle East problems.

With Soviet arms and advisers, Sadat re-equipped and re-trained Egypt's armed forces. In September 1973 he made a pact with Syria for a combined strike against Israel. Sadat chose 6 October for the attack. It was the Day of Atonement, the holiest day of prayer and fasting in the Jewish calendar. The Jews call it Yom Kippur.

### THE BAR LEV LINE

The Six-Day War brought Israel's frontier with Egypt up to the Suez Canal. To make the new frontier safe, the Israeli High Command decided to build a line of defences along the canal. They believed a defence line, together with the canal itself, would form an effective barrier to any Egyptian attack. The 150-kilometre defence line ran the entire length of the canal. General Bar Lev planned it, and the Israelis named it after him.

Soviet surface-to-air missiles supplied to Egypt brought down many Israeli aircraft along the canal.

# The Yom Kippur War (1973)

The war began in the early afternoon of 6 October. Several hundred Egyptian aircraft struck at Israeli airfields in Sinai, and massed batteries of Egyptian guns and rockets opened up on Israeli positions along the canal. By nightfall, 50,000 Egyptian troops were across the waterway and had broken through the Bar Lev line.

As the Egyptian troops began their attack, hundreds of Syrian tanks advanced on Israeli positions in the Golan Heights. The Syrian thrust pierced the Israeli line, and by midnight on 7 October the leading Syrian tanks were nearing the Israeli frontier along the River Jordan. Faced with attacks on two fronts, the Israelis chose to hit back hardest on the Syrian front, where the immediate danger was greatest. Within three days they had re-taken the Golan Heights and were moving towards the Syrian capital of Damascus. As international efforts were made to bring about a ceasefire, their advance into Syria slowed to a halt. The war became a stalemate.

## Ending the War

In Sinai, the Egyptians stopped once they had crossed the Suez Canal. The pause gave the Israelis time to bring tanks from the stalled Syrian front to face the Egyptians. On 14 October they defeated the Egyptians in a huge tank battle. Within a week, the Israelis had cut off an Egyptian army in southern Sinai. In the north, they had crossed the canal and were closing in on the Egyptian capital Cairo.

Both sides had used up huge quantities of war materials in the fighting. The Russians made good Egypt's losses, while the Americans airlifted fresh supplies to Israel.

The two superpowers had become deeply involved in

Many Israeli soldiers were away on special leave on the Day of Atonement. When the Egyptians attacked, most of the Israeli positions were short of defenders.

the conflict. In the confused and unpredictable state of the Middle East, the danger of their blundering into war with each other was growing very real. They came to the same conclusion, that the war must cease as soon as possible. The Americans put pressure on the Israelis, while the Russians used their influence with the Egyptians. On 24 October a ceasefire was declared, 17 days after the fighting had started.

The Egyptians practised the canal crossing and the assault on the Bar Lev line for three years. The real attack was skilfully carried out and took the Israelis completely by surprise.

# Ceasefire

Although the Arab states had failed to win the war they emerged from it with a new confidence in their abilities. Quite apart from a better performance on the battlefield, the Arabs had shown that they could help each other. The Arab oil-producing states had compelled the Americans to limit aid to Israel by cutting off oil supplies, and threatened to do the same to any other country proved to be helping the Israelis. They also made huge increases in

An Emergency Peace Keeping Force, raised by the United Nations from its member states, kept the two enemies apart during the five years while the peace talks were going on.

Begin (left), Carter (centre) and Sadat met for talks at Camp David in America. The peace treaty Egypt and Israel signed after the meeting ended over 30 years of war between them.

By the terms of the peace treaty, Israel withdrew from Sinai over three years and the Egyptians opened the Suez Canal to Israeli shipping.

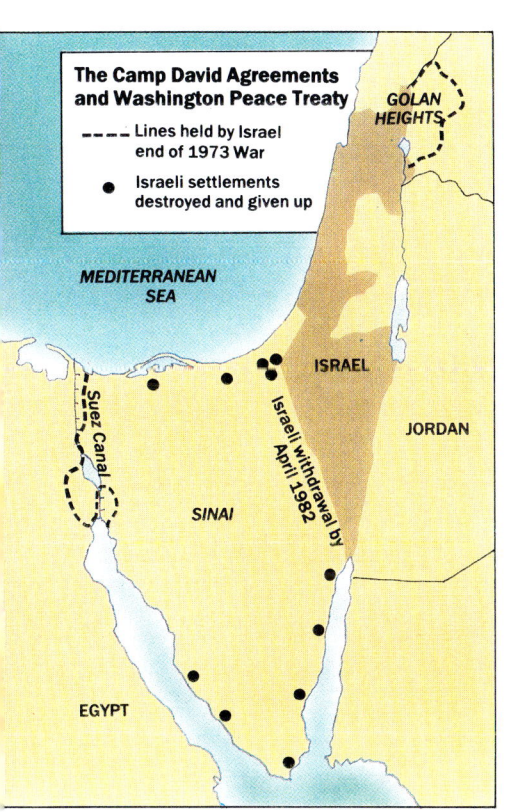

**The Camp David Agreements and Washington Peace Treaty**

- - - - Lines held by Israel end of 1973 War

• Israeli settlements destroyed and given up

GOLAN HEIGHTS

MEDITERRANEAN SEA

ISRAEL

JORDAN

Suez Canal

Israeli withdrawal by April 1982

SINAI

EGYPT

the price of their oil, and set off a world economic crisis.

The two superpowers were by now seriously alarmed. With Soviet approval, the American Secretary of State, Henry Kissinger, flew to the Middle East to begin the tortuous exercise of bringing Arabs and Israelis together.

## Peace at Last

Kissinger began peace talks by shuttling to and fro between Egypt and Israel. He got the two sides to meet for a peace conference in December 1973. Jordan joined in, but the other Arab states kept away. No agreement was reached and the meeting broke up.

Led by Kissinger, the two sides slowly edged back towards peace. In 1977 Sadat visited Israel and addressed the Israeli parliament. His bold move helped to speed the peace process. The new US president, Jimmy Carter, invited Sadat and the Israeli premier, Menachem Begin, to meet him for talks in America. After days of tough bargaining they came to an agreement. It led to a formal peace treaty in March 1979.

**The numbers of Israeli soldiers killed or wounded in the ferocious street fighting in Beirut and elsewhere grew steadily. Israeli public opinion turned against the occupation of Lebanon and forced the government to bring Israeli troops home.**

# Israel Invades Lebanon

By the end of the 1970s the main battleground between the Arabs and Israelis had shifted to Lebanon. The PLO had moved there after being driven from Jordan in Black September 1970. Their arrival had provoked a civil war between Lebanese Christians and Moslems. When it appeared that the Moslems and their PLO allies were winning the war, a Syrian force entered the fray to protect Syria's interests. At the end of 1976 Syria was occupying much of northern Lebanon, while the PLO controlled the south. From bases in this newly-gained territory, the PLO and other Arab guerilla groups launched frequent attacks across the frontier into Israel. Each raid brought savage reprisals from the Israelis upon the guerilla strongholds in the Palestinian refugee camps.

### Operation 'Peace for Galilee'

The Palestinians now possessed guns and rockets which could fire far enough to cause damage well inside Israel. The threat of these weapons proved so great that the Israelis resolved to drive the PLO out of Lebanon and set up a government friendly to Israel. Operation 'Peace for Galilee', as they called it, began on 6 June 1982.

Israeli forces advanced swiftly to the Lebanese capital Beirut and besieged it, cutting off its garrison of 10,000 Syrian troops. The United States intervened to head off a full-scale war between Israel and Syria, but the Israelis continued to hunt down the Palestinian guerillas. A United Nations force arrived to restore peace in Beirut where rival Moslem and Christian groups were at perpetual war. It failed and was withdrawn in early 1984. A year later, the Israelis pulled back to their own frontier.

For many years the Palestinians living in the Israeli-occupied territories sullenly accepted Israeli rule. In early 1988, they rose in revolt.

The uprising, or 'intifada' as the Arabs call it, has continued ever since, with periodic strikes, riots, bombings, assassinations and other acts of violence against the Israeli state.

The brutal methods sometimes used by Israeli troops have utterly failed to end the intifada; they have succeeded in drawing world attention to the Palestinian cause.

# The Future

Early this century, the British offered the Jews land in Uganda as their national home. The pioneer Zionist Theodor Herzl welcomed the proposal, but most other Zionists rejected it. Had this scheme been accepted, the 20th-century history of the Middle East (and of Central Africa) would have been very different.

At the present time, in 1991, the Middle East continues to be the most explosive and unsettled area in the world. None of the problems which have made it so have been solved. The terrible predicament of the Palestinians remains. The Israelis refuse to leave the land they occupy. War continues as the Middle East way of life.

Most of Lebanon's 800,000 refugees are Palestinians. The older people have lived in the refugee camps for 40 years, ever since they fled from the fighting in the Palestine War of 1948. Half the Palestinians in Lebanon are under 15 years of age. They have known no other life than the squalor, poverty and violence of the camps.

# Important Events of the Conflict

|  |  |
|---|---|
| 1897 | Herzl founds World Zionist Organisation. |
| 1916 | British promise Arabs their own state in Palestine. |
| 1917 | British promise to help Jews set up a Jewish homeland in Palestine. |
| 1920-21 | Jews flock to settle in Palestine. Arabs protest. Violent Arab-Jewish riots. |
| 1933 | Nazis take power in Germany. Fearsome persecution of the Jews begins. |
| 1936-39 | Arab revolt against Jewish immigration and in favour of setting up Arab state. |
| 1938 | British plan to divide Palestine between Arabs and Jews suspended. |
| 1939 | World War II breaks out. |
| 1946 | British limit Jewish immigration. Stern Gang blows up British HQ in Jerusalem. |
| 1947 | UN plan to divide Palestine rejected by Jews and Arabs. |
| 1948 | British withdraw. State of Israel proclaimed. Arabs attack. Palestine War. |
| 1949 | Arabs and Israelis sign armistice. Thousands of Arabs flee to neighbouring Arab states and create refugee problem. Continual violence along Israel's borders. |
| 1956 | Nasser nationalizes Suez Canal Company. Israel, Britain and France attack Egypt. Israelis advance to Suez. Anglo-French invasion halted by international pressure. |
| 1957 | Israel withdraws from Sinai and Gaza. |
| 1964 | PLO formed. |
| 1967 | Six-Day War. |
| 1969 | Egypt's war of attrition against Israel. |
| 1970 | Black September. PLO driven from Jordan. |
| 1973 | Yom Kippur (October) War. Israelis reverse early Arab gains and win the war. |
| 1977 | President Sadat visits Israel. |
| 1979 | After Camp David talks, Egypt and Israel sign peace treaty. |
| 1982 | Israel invades Lebanon. |
| 1985 | Israel gets out of Lebanon. |
| 1988 | Arab uprising 'the intifada' begins. |
| 1990 | Iraq occupies Kuwait. |
| 1991 | Gulf War, Saddam Hussein attacks Israel. |

# Index